M

Pick-Me-Up
and
OTHER RECIPES
from a
YORKSHIRE DALE

Mrs Hibbert's
Pick-Me-Up

and
OTHER RECIPES
from a
YORKSHIRE DALE

Joanna Moody

The
History
Press

Joanna Dawson

1930–1992

In Memoriam

First published 2010

The History Press
The Mill, Brimscombe Port
Stroud, Gloucestershire, GL5 2QG
www.thehistorypress.co.uk

British Library Cataloguing in Publication Data.
A catalogue record for this book is available from the British Library.

ISBN 978 0 7524 5728 4

Typesetting and origination by The History Press
Printed in Great Britain

Contents

List *of* Illustrations

1. Joanna Dawson © Nidderdale Museum Society

2. View of Pateley Bridge (1896), photo album vol. v of Amy Collins © Nidderdale Museum Society

3. The Metcalfe brothers ready to scythe hay, Fellbeck © Nidderdale Museum Society

4. The maypole, Summerbridge © Nidderdale Museum Society

5. Polly Skaife with hens and geese, Darley © Nidderdale Museum Society

6. A loaded haycart, Summerbridge (*c.*1910) © Nidderdale Museum Society

7. Building the haystack, Wilsill (*c.*1946–7) © Nidderdale Museum Society

8. The children's party, Methodist Manse, Dacre Banks
© Nidderdale Museum Society

9. Hostel keepers at Scar House Village (*c.* early 1930s)
© Nidderdale Museum Society

10. Birstwith Band, Hardcastle Garth (*c.* early 1900s)
© Nidderdale Museum Society

11. Mrs William Robinson on her milk float,
Glasshouses © Nidderdale Museum Society

12. Church 'Workers' Ladies, Middlesmoor
© Nidderdale Museum Society

13. Sheep washing, Stean Moor (1908)
© Nidderdale Museum Society

14. Map of Nidderdale, showing place-names mentioned
© Nidderdale Area of Outstanding Natural Beauty

Drawings by Sheila Hone
© Nidderdale Museum Society

Preface

Mrs Hibbert's Pick-Me-Up and the other 101 recipes and handy hints included here come from a valuable collection of primary source material now lodged in the archives of the Nidderdale Museum, at Pateley Bridge in the Yorkshire Dales. It belonged to Joanna Dawson, who was a Methodist Local Preacher, an experienced dairy farmer and a keen historian of Nidderdale.

With others she shared a deep concern for the traditional way of life which seemed to be disappearing rapidly from the dale after the Second World War. Farms were adopting new methods, the former lead and stone industries had collapsed and families were becoming dispersed. In 1975 she was a founder of the Nidderdale Museum, set up by volunteers to display the rich and varied local heritage. As a result of their enthusiasm and formidable organisation a flourishing Society was formed: 'to advance the education of the public by maintaining a museum in the Nidderdale area to collect, preserve and exhibit items of archaeological, historical, industrial, educational and community interest'. In 1990 it was given the National Heritage Museum of the Year Award for 'The Museum which does the most with the least.'

Travelling around Nidderdale with indefatigable energy Joanna garnered from the people she encountered stories, anecdotes and knowledge of the dale's customs and methods. Her unbounded interest led to a vast collection of unsorted and unclassified information which she planned to tackle when she retired. But, only a few months before that, she was found to be terminally ill. She asked that her friends at the museum should undertake the task and eventually publish her work.

We are pleased to honour the pledge we gave her and offer this collection in tribute to a dedicated public servant, a great enthusiast, and a dear friend to many in the dale.

Anna Donnelly
Secretary, Nidderdale Museum Society

Profile *of* Joanna Mary Grylls Dawson

My sister Joanna was born in Huddersfield in 1930, the oldest of a family of five. At the time, the whole family lived with our grandfather. In 1939 our father took over the tenancy of Winsley Grange Farm, Hartwith, in Nidderdale, and from 1941 this became our main home. Joanna continued her education at Greenhead High School in Huddersfield, staying with Grandfather during the week. On Monday mornings she made the long journey by public transport, walking two miles to Birstwith railway station, then by train or bus, and returned Fridays the same way. The school agreed that she may arrive at 10 a.m. provided that she undertook the work of the first lesson at home. At weekends and holidays she worked on the farm, joined the Pateley Bridge Young Farmers Club and showed her calf at the Nidderdale Agricultural Show. Later she took part in all YFC activities, such as

1. Joanna Dawson.

cattle judging and other competitions at local shows.

After gaining the equivalent of three good A-levels in her Higher School Certificate and being called for interview at Cambridge University, where our mother had been a student, Joanna chose to turn her back on higher education and elected to help run the farm with our parents. However she did keep in touch with her history teacher and school friends for the rest of her life.

Joanna shared the management of the prize-winning British Friesian 'Winyates' herd built up by our father. She was responsible for the paperwork concerning the pedigree calves, and every calf required its markings to be carefully sketched in duplicate in black and white and sent off for registration (no ear clips in those days). She frequently took the cattle to local markets, washed them and showed them in the ring. She gradually took over the garden and home cooking, and at various local shows displayed cakes, preserves and flower arrangements (using chicken wire to support the flowers as there was no oasis then either).

Joanna became involved within the Women's Institute, qualifying as a produce guild judge and officiating in this capacity at many shows. She served on the WI County Committee for a number of years and worked tirelessly as a member of its panel of lecturers travelling the county and further afield.

Joanna's religion was central to her life and she trained as a very active local preacher in the Pateley Bridge circuit of the Methodist Church and within the wider district. Her outgoing nature allowed her to enjoy fellowship with members of all Christian denominations, which led to much happiness for all involved. She had a real affection for children and was always willing to help anyone in need, spending hours with the lonely, sick and elderly. Many of her friends frequently stated what a real pleasure it was to be in her company. She never faulted in duties asked of her, which included pastoral visiting, being the local preachers' secretary and a representative at Methodist Synod and conferences.

In 1978 at the Annual Methodist Conference in Bradford Joanna presented the Annual Wesley Historical lecture, her subject being the Methodist history within the 'Great Haworth Round'. As it was Joanna giving the lecture on their chapels and their families, Methodists came by coach from afar to hear her and the Wells Road Methodist Church was crowded out.

In about 1962 the family moved to Hardcastle Garth. Another of Joanna's interests was local history, possibly because of the old Quaker burial ground situated on the farm. She soon developed into a popular and proficient lecturer on diverse subjects including local history, Quakerism, herbs and spices and so forth, particularly for special events such as chapel centenaries and Women's Institutes, and she published booklets emphasising the importance of the local families involved. She wrote a number of other small books and articles, mainly connected with Methodism, and also supplied the material, if not always the writing, for several long series in the *Nidderdale Herald*, although she was not always acknowledged for her contribution. Following a trip with me to Portsmouth to see the wreck of the *Mary Rose*, she developed a particular interest in the ancient ship and became an established lecturer for the *Mary Rose* Trust.

Through her farming and religious activities Joanna travelled up and down Nidderdale, getting to know the older people and learning their life stories. As many were Methodists she rapidly became an expert. Her knowledge of local Methodism, the chapel and churches and the families of Nidderdale was unsurpassed. And after becoming a guide for Fountains Abbey she extended her range to include the whole of Yorkshire.

Rosemary Randerson (née Dawson) and others

An Appreciation

Joanna Dawson and I first met in September 1958 at the opening of Bernard Jennings' local history class. She quickly established herself as one of its most enthusiastic members, with a deep knowledge of agriculture and Methodism. When the Nidderdale WEA Branch was formed, she was its first chairman – with Marjorie Light as treasurer and me as secretary; we were the youngest branch officials in the District. We quickly became friends, and she was a welcome visitor at all times – we had long talks, often into the small hours, about our interests and personal lives.

She was an important member of our local history class, and the subsequent research and publication of *A History of Nidderdale* (1967) benefited from her encyclopaedic knowledge. Her friendship with people throughout the dale meant that she was able to access knowledge and documents which would not be revealed to casual enquirers. Joanna was someone who made copious notes, regrettably often on scrappy bits of paper, in minute handwriting – a nightmare to decipher because she abhorred tape recorders and typewriters – but these she bequeathed to Nidderdale Museum, and they form a wonderful resource of background information, gleaned from individuals and archives around the county. She also donated her extensive library of local history books, many of them very rare and valuable.

She was a founder member of the museum, and served on the committee for several years, until pressure of her other activities meant she had to resign. During her last year, however, she had resumed helping as a steward, and was looking forward to doing much more once she had fully retired.

Having sold the last of her cattle on the previous Monday, preparatory to retiring, Joanna was diagnosed with terminal cancer in January 1992. When I visited her in hospital a few days later, she had already organised her will, her nursing care and her funeral, and she faced her illness with a calm, contented and confident faith. Whilst in the nursing home at Killinghall she had a constant queue of visitors from all over the north.

She died three months later, on Easter Sunday morning, aged sixty-one. 'What a glorious Easter Day for her!' said the minister at her funeral. The mourners at the celebration of her life overflowed the Summerbridge Chapel and its annexe – a great tribute to an admired and much loved lady.

I still miss her.

Eileen Burgess

Editorial Note

Not long after Joanna Dawson died her notes were sorted and referenced for the museum archives by Eileen Burgess, who also began to type them out. Her work on this, however, was interrupted by other publications, and it was not until the summer of 2008 that she asked me if I would like to take on a small project from 'another Joanna' and start again.

I was enchanted by what I found. Here was a celebrated local historian, an enthusiastic traveller and a welcome visitor into people's homes – a 'squirrel' collector of miscellaneous information, all of which offered an illuminating and endearing insight into the domestic story of Nidderdale. Amongst the papers I discovered a fragrant scene from the farmhouse kitchens of long ago, when large teas and suppers featured as the reward for a hard-working rural life, where the wives by their ranges had skills and knowledge to be learned and passed on through the generations, and when events such as chapel outings, sheep washing, hay-making, and the maypole, brought them joyfully together to share recipes and hints amongst themselves.

Some of these are perhaps not forgotten, but others I felt might be and, besides, behind them all was a way of life that formed part of the rich heritage of this lovely dale, designated in 1994 as an Area of Outstanding Natural Beauty.

Everyone remembers Joanna Dawson with considerable warmth, affection and respect, and her impressive note-taking was legendary. This collection is thus transcribed from many handwritten jottings on cards, odd scraps of paper, and pages torn from the notebooks she must have constantly carried with her. She copied the poems down as she listened to them being remembered, recited and read, and she recorded a background commentary to locate the recipes in their context. I have left this in its entirety, and I hope those who knew her will find that her own distinctive voice comes through. My occasional editorial interventions are clearly marked inside square brackets.

The illustrations are from the museum's extensive photographic archive, and have been chosen to give a small pictorial record of the folk who, decades ago, cooked and enjoyed these recipes. They vary from the dale's men and women who provided the wherewithal from their farms, to the Church 'Workers' of Middlesmoor, the children in Dacre and Summerbridge, the Birstwith Band, and to the lively hostel keepers who cooked for the navvies building the great Scar dam and reservoir in Upper Nidderdale. The drawings by Sheila Hone depict a selection from the museum's collection of kitchen equipment once used by Nidderdale housewives, including brass kettles and pans, stone jars, an invalid beaker, and a Lovefeast cup.

Some of the recipes assume a basic knowledge of an older style of cooking, and the occasional lack of instruction is typical in its assumption of knowledge already in place. Joanna's sister, Rosemary, remembers that they only had the fireside oven of the coal-fired range until Joanna was about nineteen, and they used to put a hand inside to test how hot it was and stoke the fire accordingly. Hence the recipes do not necessarily include a stated temperature – they tend to rely on experience, guess work and common sense. The cook adjusted the temperature of the oven by means of flues and dampers, and until she could gauge the temperature by experience she may have used Mrs Blacker's method:

> If a sheet of paper burns when thrown in, the oven is too
>   hot.
> When the paper becomes dark brown, it is suitable for
>   pastry.
> When light brown, it does pies.
> When dark yellow, it does cakes.
> When the paper is light yellow, use the oven for pud-
>   dings, biscuits and small pastry.

Keeping the range clean and well black-leaded was the bane of many a woman's life, but it was the centre of the home and the brass and copper surrounding it

2.View of Pateley Bridge (1896).

were kept carefully polished and shining to catch the light and brighten up the dark fireplace. A kettle would have hung from the reckon (crook *or* hook) in the chimney, cast iron pans and griddles would have been ready for use, and saucepans and ladling cans must have been to hand.

These recipes include seasonal dishes and sweet and savoury teas, suppers and field lunches; there are delicious hedgerow conserves and pickles, and refreshing fruit and temperance beverages, along with some useful household advice drawn from age-old wisdom. They are here for their historical and local interest – such as the redoubtable Mrs Hibbert's Pick-Me-Up, wherein you pour half a breakfastcupful of boiling water on as much cayenne pepper as would lie on an old threepenny piece, sweeten to taste, and then add a good quantity of milk or cream. They are organised mainly to follow the seasons from Shrovetide in early spring to the end of the year, where they close with invalid remedies to set you up for the rigours of a long cold winter. Not all have been recently tested, so please be very careful if using any unusual ingredients: we cannot be held responsible for any accidents or unforeseen reactions which may occur as a result of trying them out.

The sources of many recipes are not given in Joanna's notes, but we have made every effort to trace their origins. Certain individuals are mentioned, and there are a few brief references to publications of the former Yorkshire Federation of Women's Institutes, with which Joanna was closely involved before it was divided out into separate regions; these are indicated where appropriate. If we have unintentionally infringed copyright, or should have asked permission for an item, we unreservedly apologise, and will make the adjustment in any future edition.

Joanna Moody

Acknowledgements

Our grateful thanks are due to Rosemary Randerson (*née* Dawson), Shirley Dawson, Christine Harker, Dinah Lee, and Stan Beer for responding helpfully to requests for information, and to Andrea Ives for background detail; to Paul Burgess at Nidderdale Area of Outstanding Natural Beauty; to John Bass (former Chairman), Sue Hickson (Treasurer) and the Committee of the Nidderdale Museum Society; and to Brian Ives for his technical expertise.

RECIPES

Advice to Wives

Occupy yourself chiefly with household affairs,
and do not trouble yourself with other matters,
or offer suggestions and advice to your husband
until he asks for them.

Nidderdale Olminac, 1868

Shrovetide in Nidderdale

Each day in Shrovetide week was known by its own peculiar name: Collop Monday, for eggs and collops (an old word for thick slices of meat); Shrove or Pancake Tuesday; Fritter or Frutas Wednesday; Bloody Thorsday, for black puddings.

At Shrovetide we used to make a special treat called fritters. They were composed of all kinds of dried fruit, sugar, flour, a good lot of eggs and yeast, warm milk – mix[ed] all together to a batter and left to rise up then fried them up in a frying pan in our own pig lard. We used to measure it with a cup the size of a small crumpet and turned over until brown. They would keep a few weeks and were good either cold or warmed like toast.

Memories of Sarah Ann Carling née Beecroft (b.1879) of Westfield

❧ *Shrovetide Pateley Fritters (i)* ❧

¾ oz yeast

1 pt warm milk

12 oz flour

1 oz lard

3 oz currants

1½ oz raisins

a little lemon peel if liked

1 tablespoon sugar

salt spoon cinnamon

salt spoon salt

1 large apple chopped finely

Crumble the yeast into a little of the warm milk and let it rise. Warm the flour in a bowl. Melt the lard in the remainder of the milk. Pour the yeast into the centre of the flour, add the lard and milk and let it rise a few minutes longer. Add the rest of the ingredients and beat to a stiff batter. Let it rise in a warm place for one hour.

Heat a little dripping or lard in a frying pan, put in the batter in large spoonsful and when well browned underneath turn over and cook on the other side till brown.

[JD notes 'WI recipe']

❧ *Pateley Fritters (ii)* ❧

1 oz yeast

1 teaspoon sugar

dash of pepper

2 lb flour

1 lb sugar

¼ lb currants

¼ lb sultanas

2 eggs

pinch of salt

a little grated nutmeg

warm milk

Mix the yeast with a teaspoon of sugar and a dash of pepper. Mix all the other ingredients together, make a well in the centre and add the yeast and enough warm milk or milk and water to make a soft mixture rather thicker than a Yorkshire Pudding batter. Let it rise in a warm place for a few hours, then drop in tablespoonfuls at a time into a hot greased frying pan. When brown on one side, turn over and cook on the reverse.

Eggs

Eggs become plentiful at Whitsuntide and so does milk as the cows are turned out on to the hillside pastures after the long Nidderdale winter. A traditional delicacy found on the tea table, along with a wonderful variety of assorted baking, are custard tarts.

❀ *Baked Custard Tarts* ❀

Short crust pastry   4 eggs
1 pint milk   1 tablespoon sugar

Line a deep pie dish with short crust pastry, pressing it well in. Beat the eggs well and add the sugar, then the milk and stir well together. Pour into the pastry and bake in a fairly hot oven for 15 minutes, then reduce the heat to moderate and bake until the custard is set (about another half hour). Make sure the fat is well rubbed into the flour for the pastry, otherwise this will rise to the top of the custard.

❧ *Pateley Omelette* ❧

Chop a small onion very fine, add pepper, salt, a little sage or parsley, 1 egg and 2 tablespoons of milk. Fry in hot dripping until done, turn half over and serve.

This came from Mrs Green of Pateley – the Greens appear in the Pateley Church registers from the 1720s. Thomas Green was a great friend of John Wesley and entertained him in his house up Old Church Lane on several occasions. He was a skilled builder and carpenter, and built the first two chapels in Pateley Bridge, one adjoining his house, and then the 1776-1908 chapel on the site of the present one. He also restored Middlesmoor Church in the 1770s.

Haytime

The Dales economy depends on a good hay time. Every new Minister coming into Nidderdale realises that the busy round of weeknight chapel meetings has to cease completely from mid-June till the start of the Harvest Festivals of which Heathfield, the first week in September, is the first.

3. The Metcalfe brothers ready to scythe hay, Fellbeck.

Mowing starts at dawn and work goes on until after dark. Dales weather is very unpredictable.

Farmers' wives and daughters are kept busy taking 'drinkings' to the fields – drinks as well as food are prepared and stored on the stone slabs of the old farmhouse larders.

❧ *Elderflower Champagne* ❧

A delicious and popular drink for hot summer days and hay time.

1½ lb sugar	1 gallon cold water
2 lemons	4 heads of elderflowers
2 tablespoons white wine vinegar	

Put all ingredients except the lemons into a large bowl; squeeze the lemons and quarter them and add to the other ingredients. Stand for 24 hours, stirring occasionally. Strain and bottle into screw-top bottles. The 'champagne' will be ready for drinking in a few days.

TRUE FRIENDSHIP

True friendship unfeigned
Doth rest unrestrained,
   No terror can tame it:
Not gaining or losing,
Nor gallant gay glossing,
   Can ever reclaim it.
In pain, and in pleasure,
The most truest treasure
   That may be desired,
Is loyal love deemed,
Of wisdom esteemed
   And chiefly required.

When the men and women came in at dark from the hay-field it was the custom to sit down to a good supper of boiled bacon, cold beef and a hot savoury dish, followed by fruit pie and cheese.

❈ *Bishopside Supper Dish* ❈

Take 1 large onion, ¼ [lb] cheese, 1 tablespoon milk. Chop the onion fairly small, grate the cheese and mix in a basin with the milk, pinch of salt and pepper. Line a large plate with pastry, put in the cheese and onion, cover with more pastry. Bake in a moderate oven. Can be eaten either hot or cold.

A savoury dish from Pateley Bridge Church
Restoration Fund Book, 1924

❀ *Potato and Onion Balls* ❀

Boil a Spanish onion till soft, whip it up well with 4 times its volume of mashed potato. Moisten with butter, cream or milk. Season, salt and pepper, bind with egg yolks. Roll into balls, egg and breadcrumbs, and fry in deep fat.

❀ *Potato Cake* ❀

4 oz flour	4 oz mashed potato
4 oz butter	3 oz sugar
1 egg	little milk

Beat the butter and sugar, add beaten egg, then flour and potato, using a little milk. Turn into a greased cake tin and bake for ½ hour. Split open, spread well with butter, sprinkle with sugar. Serve hot.

❧ *Crusty Cheese Bake* ❧

5 thin slices white bread	2 oz cheddar cheese, grated
2 oz ham, chopped	1 oz mushrooms, peeled and
2 eggs	sliced
1 pint milk	1 level teaspoon dry mustard

Cut each slice of bread into 4. Fill greased ovenproof dish with a layer of bread, 1 oz cheese, mushrooms and ham. Finish with a layer of bread. Sprinkle with rest of cheese. Beat eggs with mustard. Gradually add milk and whisk together. Pour over bread. Bake in centre of a moderate oven for 45 minutes or till golden and puffy. Garnish with grilled mushrooms. Serve hot with a green salad or hot green vegetables.

Mushrooms

August and September was mushroom time. Mushrooms used to grow in abundance in Nidderdale in the days of horses, and before artificial fertilisers and reseeding of pastures became common.

The Houseman family of Hartwith recalls scores of baskets being dropped off the train at all the halts sent by Bradford wholesalers. Whole families rose at 4 a.m. and the 7 a.m. train went down with the luggage van absolutely full of fresh picked mushrooms; it was chaos on Monday mornings when each station was full of baby calves in sacks going to Knaresborough and Otley markets.

❧ *Boiled Mushrooms* ❧

Take good-sized mushrooms, thick and firm. Peel, wash and drain. Steep 2 hours in salad oil, pepper and salt. Then put on a gridiron and broil over a clear fire. Turn to get done on both sides. When done put on a dish. Serve with a sauce made thus: put into a stewpan some chopped parsley and a very little chopped onion and salad oil and a little lemon juice or vinegar pour over the mushrooms and serve very hot.

A popular Dales supper dish, eighteenth century, from an old almanac.

Lovefeasts

Lovefeasts, established by John Wesley, were days on which Methodists from around a local area gathered in open chapel to reaffirm and strengthen their commitment to their faith. Special and lively preachers were engaged for lengthy services, when appropriate hymns were sung and testimony could be given by any of the members present. Wesley once said that the 'Very design is free and familiar, everyone has liberty to speak whatever may be to the glory of God. The flame ran from heart to heart; one told how my morning sermon had set her heart at liberty.'

To sustain them during the long service, and probably to remind them of the Last Supper, Lovefeast bread was handed round, together with a large two-handled loving cup, first filled with ale but later with water.

Each area had its own particular recipe, with the oldest being based on the traditional yeast mixture which was the foundation of all celebration cakes before the advent of baking powder in the mid 19th century. These recipes, however, are all baking powder adaptations – quicker and more reliable than the yeast versions.

❧ *Middlesmoor Lovefeast Cake* ❧

2 lbs flour	5 oz fresh butter
1 lb sugar	5 oz lard
1 lb currants	½ lb sultanas
¼ lb lemon peel	2 oz baking powder
3 eggs	1 pint of milk
spices to taste	

Mix flour and baking powder. Rub in the butter, add the fruit. Beat the eggs with the milk and dry ingredients. Put into loaf tins and bake in a moderate oven.

Miss Brown, Ramsgill, 1903

❧ *Pateley Bridge Lovefeast Bread* ❧

2 lbs flour	1 pint of milk
1 lb butter	2 eggs
1 lb sugar	2 oz baking powder
¼ lb lemon peel	currants & sultanas if desired

Method as Middlesmoor.

Mrs C Grainge, Otley

❧ *Laverton and Pateley Lovefeast Bread* ❧

2½ lb flour
7 oz lard
1 teaspoon bicarbonate of soda
1 lb fruit and peel.

9 oz sugar
1 oz yeast

Nutmeg and salt and spice to
taste.

❧ *Lovefeast Cake of the Verity and Simpson Families* ❧

2 lbs flour
1½ lb sugar
1 lb sultanas
pinch salt
6 eggs
a little milk

1 lb butter
1 lb currants
2 oz lemon peel
2 oz ground almonds
3 teaspoons baking powder

The children had their celebrations. The annual Sunday School Treat usually involved a procession of teachers and scholars to the home of a local worthy – in Pateley Bridge, either Castlestead (George Metcalfe) for Methodists or Bewerley Hall (Squire Yorke) for Anglicans. There they would sing hymns, have races and enjoy the gardens, plus tea.

4. The maypole, Summerbridge.

❧ *Sunday School Treat Cakes* ❧

3 lbs flour
1½ lbs sugar
¼ lb lemon peel
1 pint new milk

2 lbs currants
1 lb butter
10 eggs
2 tablespoons baking powder

Oatcakes

Because of the wet climate in the upper dale, the only cereal crop which could ripen was oats. Each farm had a small plot of arable for growing sufficient for the family's needs. In the old days, oats were ground to meal in the stone querns and blended with a little fat and water into a paste, then patted out and baked on the hearth stone. Farmers' wives made as many as 15 dozen. They were eaten with white cheese and a light home-brewed beer.

Built-in bakstones were common in Nidderdale. Lucas's Studies in Nidderdale (1878) mentions clapcake, riddle cake, held-on cake and turned-down cake, of which the last three were made by pouring into a bakstone. Mrs J. Beckwith (b. 1873) talked of using a round piece of brown paper for throwing the batter on to a girdle at New Houses in Upper Nidderdale.

Oatmeal was mixed with water in a wooden trough or 'knade-kit', poured onto a wooden board or 'bak-brade' and covered with muslin. From this it was transferred to the 'bak-stone', by the side of the fire grate (which was always kept hot, for simmering stews etc). After a few seconds it was turned with a wooden 'spittle', then whilst still moist it was hung over a 'bread creel' or 'bread fleak' to dry.

NB. Bakstones were often fixed to a metal frame, and could be used over the fire.

Men worked for long hours on oatcake and cheese without lacking endurance and strength.

When a batch of oatcakes was ready, they were sometimes stored on an 'oatfleak'- a rack suspended from the beams often later used as a clothes airer – to protect them from vermin. They dried, and pieces could be broken off as needed. [In JD's collection are extracts on oatcakes from Hartley & Ingleby Life and Tradition in the Yorkshire Dales (1956)].

Three Dales Plain Oatcakes

❧ *(i) Oatcake or Haverbread* ❧

½ pint milk

½ pint water

2 saltspoons salt

6 heaped tablespoons fine oatmeal

3 heaped tablespoons flour

1 oz yeast

Mix together the dry ingredients, warm milk and water, crumble in the yeast, and let it stand 20 minutes. Cook in a lard-greased frying pan, turn when brown, and cook on the other side.

[JD notes 'Mrs Appleby (Dalesman)']

❧ *(ii) Oatcakes to Serve With Cheese* ❧

½ best medium oatmeal

pinch bicarbonate soda

1 oz butter

½ teaspoon table salt

¼ pint milk

Put butter in saucepan with milk, stir in other ingredients, mix well. Put on floured board, roll quickly very thin, cut with cutter, bake 3 or 4 minutes, moderate oven. Goes crisp when cold.

Miss Alice Simpson, Covill House, 1907

❀ *(iii) Oatcake* ❀

7 oz oats	2 oz flour
3 oz butter	3 oz sugar
½ teaspoon baking powder	1 egg

Roll out.

❀ *Fruit Oatcake* ❀

2 oz chopped dates	2 oz chopped raisins or sultanas
4 oz porridge oats	4 oz self-raising flour
4 oz margarine	4 oz sugar
a little spice	

Heat dates with a little water till soft. Rub fat into flour and oats and spices. Add sugar and mix to stiff dough. Divide into ½ and roll out to fit 2 sandwich tins. Spread with fruit mixture. Cover with other ½. Bake 20 minutes.

5. Polly Skaife with hens and geese, Darley.

An havverceeake Nell left her backstan an' bread
Convinced 'at oade Tim had geeane rang in hiz heead
Oade bandy leg'd Dicky wer stop-thacking t'hoose
An sueger tung'd Mary were mucking her goose.

From *T'Deeacre Pig Hunt*

❧ *Clap Cake* ❧

*Old Danish Klappe-brod – these are thin cakes, beaten with
the hand. A recipe which probably goes back to Viking times,
with baking powder being used to make a lighter mixture,
another variation on the oatcake recipe.*

1¾ lb medium oatmeal	¾ lb flour
10 oz lard	1 teaspoon salt
4 teaspoons baking powder	1 gill milk

Mix altogether, roll out and cut in squares. Bake in a
moderate oven.

Mrs Ben Skaife, Darley, née *Alice Mawer, Ramsgill*

Mestyng Bread
½ wheat ½ rye

Mestlyng Bread
½ rye ½ barley

❦ *Pateley Pepper Cake* ❦

Pepper was sometimes used to speed up the action of the yeast, so the pepper cakes were probably again yeast based originally.

12 oz plain flour
12 oz black treacle
4 oz butter
2 beaten eggs

4 oz soft brown sugar
½ oz ground cloves
½ teaspoon bicarbonate of soda

Rub the fat into the flour, add the sugar, spices, then the bicarbonate of soda mixed with a little milk, the treacle and the eggs. Mix well, put into a suitable, well greased tin and bake at Gas 4 (350°F) for about an hour.

❦ *Lower Nidd Valley Pepper Cake* ❦

1½ lb flour
1 oz powdered cloves
½ lb butter

½ lb moist brown sugar
1½ lb treacle
5 well-beaten eggs

1 teaspoon pearl ash melted in a little milk

Mix all together with the eggs and bake at 350°F (Mark 4) for 2 hours.

A little bit of Pepper Cake,
A little bit of cheese,
A cup of cold water
And a penny if you please.

❀ *Ginger Loaf* ❀

1 lb flour	1 lb treacle
4 oz butter	Candied peel cut fine
a few caraway seeds powdered fine	1 teaspoon bicarbonate of soda

Butter and treacle to be made milk-warm and the flour to be mixed in gradually. The soda to be put in last dissolved in a little milk – let it stand ½ hour to rise, bake in slow oven.

Pateley, 1885

❀ *Ginger Biscuits* ❀

10 oz flour	2 teaspoons ground ginger
4 oz lard	3 tablespoons golden syrup
4 oz sugar	½ teaspoon bicarbonate of soda

Beat lard and sugar together, add syrup (warmed), flour and ginger. Dissolve soda in a little water, work all into a stiff dough. Pull off pieces size of a walnut, roll into balls with the hand. Bake on a well-greased tin 350°F (moderate oven).

Mrs Lumley, Hartwith

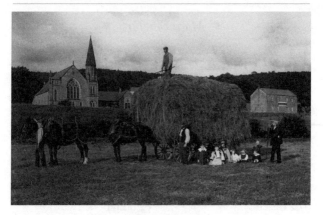

6. A loaded haycart, Summerbridge (c.1910).

❧ *Gingerbread* ❧

½ lb self-raising flour	3 oz margarine and lard mixed
2 oz Demerara sugar	½ lb golden syrup
2 oz glace cherries	2 teaspoons ground ginger
1 egg	3 good tablespoons milk

Mix flour, sugar and ginger, add chopped cherries and the beaten egg, then the melted fat and syrup and milk to make a soft mixture. Pour into a tin 10ins by 8ins and bake in the oven for 45 minutes. 350°F for 10 minutes, then turn down to 325°.

❧ Macaroon Tarts ❧

¾ oz cornflour	½ oz butter
4 oz caster sugar	4 oz ground almonds
1 egg	3 tablespoons jam

❧ Brandy Snaps ❧

6 oz flour	6 oz sugar
6 oz treacle	5 oz butter

Wet your fingers in cold water and pat the brandy snap on the tin to make it go thin and holey.

Curd tarts were a feature in the summer, when the cows had calved and were yielding generously. Traditionally served at Whitsuntide, they were sometimes called cheesecakes, and were appreciated on special occasions by the navvies living in hostels where they were building Scar House dam and reservoir in Upper Nidderdale.

❧ Yorkshire Curd Tarts ❧

8 oz curds	a small knob of butter (melted)
2 eggs	a little grated lemon rind
4 oz sugar	a pinch of nutmeg
2 oz currants	

Mix curds with fruit and flavourings. Beat eggs well and stir in with the sugar and butter. Bake in a moderate oven.

❧ *Yorkshire Curd Cheese Tarts* ❧

3 oz butter	1 hard boiled egg, chopped
3 oz sugar	1 dessertspoon ground rice
3 oz currants	½ teaspoon nutmeg

Cream butter and sugar, add currants, egg and ground rice and nutmeg. Bake in a moderate oven.

❧ *Yorkshire Fruit Loaves* ❧

1 lb self-raising flour	¼ teaspoon salt
½ margarine- butter used	½ lb sugar
¼ pt. milk	½ teaspoon bicarbonate of soda
½ lb currants	½ lb sultanas
¼ lb mixed peel	2 eggs

Sieve flour with salt, rub in margarine. Stir in sugar and cleaned fruit. Dissolve bicarbonate of soda in a little milk. Stir in eggs, bicarb. and enough milk to make a chopping consistency. Put into 2 or 3 loaf tins. Bake 35–40 minutes in a moderate oven.

[JD notes 'p.65 current W. I. Recipe book']

Brimham Rocks Scripture Cake

Scripture cakes were quite a feature of chapel & church cook-
ery books in the 19th century. [Chapel outings were and still
are a feature of the Dales. The following was a contribution by
JD to a Methodist publication].

The ladies of former days kept mainly in the background,
singing at 'Fruit Banquets' where trays of fruit were passed
round at frequent intervals. On one occasion they fed fifteen
hundred Wesleyan Methodists in a marquee on Brimham
Rocks in the rain, baking all the bread themselves. From these
days there survives a recipe for a Scripture Cake. Why not try
to bake this cake yourself, ladies? J. D.

4½ cups of 1 Kings IV, 22; 1½ cups of Judges V, 25 last
clause; 1 cup of Numbers XVII, 8; 2 cups of Jeremiah
VI, 20; 2 cups of 1 Samuel XXX, 12 second clause; 2
cups of Nahum III, 12; 2 tablespoons 1 Samuel XIV, 25.
Season to taste with 2 Chronicles IX, 9; six of Jeremiah
XVII, 11; a piece of Leviticus II, 13; ½ cup of Judges
IV, 19 latter part; 2 tablespoons of Amos IV, 5. Follow
Solomon's prescription of correct training of a youth.
Proverbs XXIII, 14. Add a little baking powder. In
measuring quantities, remember Proverbs XI, 25.

[In the Holy Bible, Authorised Version:
4½ cups of 1 Kings 4: 22 – 'And Solomon's provision for one
day was thirty measures of fine flour, and threescore measures
of meal.'

7. Building the haystack, Wilsill (c. 1946–7).

1½ cups of Judges 5: 25 – 'she brought forth butter in a lordly dish.'
1 cup of Numbers 17: 8 – '… and, behold the rod of Aaron …brought forth buds, and bloomed blossoms, and yielded almonds.'
2 cups of Jeremiah 6: 20 – 'To what purpose cometh there to me incense from Sheba, and the sweet cane {sugar} from a far country.'
2 cups of 1 Samuel 30: 12 – 'And they gave him a piece of a cake of figs, and two clusters of raisins.'
2 cups of Nahum 3: 12 – 'All thy strong holds shall be like fig trees with the first ripe figs {dried figs}: if they be shaken, they shall even fall into the mouth of the eater.'

2 tablespoons 1 Samuel 14: 25 – 'And all they of the land came to a wood; and there was honey upon the ground.'

Season to taste with 2 Chronicles 9: 9 – 'And she gave the king a hundred and twenty talents of gold, and of spices great abundance, and precious stones.'

Six of Jeremiah 17: 11 – 'As the partridge sitteth on eggs, and hatcheth them not; so he that getteth riches, and not by right, shall leave them in the midst of his days, and at his end shall be a fool.'

A piece of Leviticus 2: 13 – 'And every oblation of thy meat offering shalt thou season with salt.'

½ cup of Judges 4: 19 – 'And she opened a bottle of milk, and gave him drink, and covered him…'

2 tablespoons of Amos 4: 5 – 'And offer a thanksgiving with leaven'{-er, such as baking soda}.

Follow Solomon's prescription of correct training of a youth, Proverbs 23:14 – 'Thou shalt beat him with the rod, and shalt deliver his soul from hell.'

Add a little baking powder.

In measuring quantities, remember Proverbs 11: 25 - 'The liberal soul shall be made fat: and he that watereth shall be watered also himself.' The Holy Bible New International Version has: 'A generous person will prosper; whoever refreshes others will be refreshed.'

There are no instructions for baking.]

❦ *Picnic Honey Cake* ❦

4 oz butter	1 teaspoon baking powder
8 oz caster sugar	½ teaspoon nutmeg
3 eggs	2 tablespoons honey
6 oz flour	8 oz walnuts
¼ teaspoon salt	2 tablespoons milk
1 lb seedless raisins	¼ teaspoon bicarbonate of soda

Cream butter and sugar, add eggs, flour and milk, then
honey, walnuts and raisins.
Bake 350°F for 2½ hours.

❦ *Orange Cake* ❦

2 eggs	their weight in flour and sugar
2 oz butter	1 orange
1 small teaspoon baking powder	

Beat the butter to a cream, add the sugar and beat again,
then add flour, orange rind grated, baking powder and
½ the juice of the orange. Bake in a moderate oven for
½ hour. Ice the cake as soon as it comes out of the oven
tin with 4 oz icing sugar and remaining ½ orange juice
mixed together.

❧ *Economy Hint* ❧

Break crusts of bread into bits, pour boiling water on them, soak 5 minutes, drain off the water, mash fine, stir into batter or cake mixtures, it lightens them.

❀ *Date Scones* ❀

12 oz wholemeal flour	1 egg
4 oz dates	salt
2 oz sugar	2 oz butter
milk	

❀ *Apple Scones* ❀

2 medium cooking apples	1 lb self-raising flour
1 teaspoon salt	2 level teaspoons baking powder
4 oz butter	4 oz caster sugar
scant ½ pint cold milk	1 tablespoon sieved apricot jam

Peel, core and finely chop one apple. Sift together flour, salt and baking powder. Rub in butter, then add caster sugar and chopped apple. Mix to a soft but not sticky dough with milk. Roll out 6 to 8 inch circle, about 1½ inches thick, on floured baking sheet. Mark top into 8 wedges. Peel and core remaining apple and cut into thin slices. Brush top of scone with milk and arrange apple slices on top. Bake in a moderately hot oven for about 30 minutes. While still hot brush apple slices with apricot jam. Serve warm with butter.

❧ *Treacle Scones* ❧

½ oz flour
1½ oz sugar
4 tablespoons milk
1 teaspoon carbonate soda

1½ oz butter
1 tablespoon treacle
1 teaspoon cream of tartar
1 teaspoon cinnamon

Dissolve treacle in milk, mix butter and flour, add treacle and milk, stir till fairly stiff. Cut fairly thickly.

Poem Recited By An 82 Year Old In 1869

The wimmin seem quite different
Fra wat they used to be;
Tho' bread were broon, they fain sat down
An' made a hearty tea.
They noo appear fatigued, oh dear!
If they the hoose sud sweep
Ner do they spare the rockin' chare
To rock themselves to sleep.

❧ *Brown Scones* ❧

6 oz brown flour
a pinch of salt
2 oz butter
milk

2 oz white flour
2 teaspoons baking powder
2 tablespoons sugar

Mix altogether. Bake 10 minutes.

❧ *Scotch Shortbread* ❧

5 oz flour
2½ oz ground rice

4 oz butter
2 oz sugar

Knead well. Bake 15 mins.

❧ *Cornflour Buns* ❧

Beat 6 oz butter to a cream. 3 eggs well beaten 6 oz of
sugar 4 oz corn flour 4 oz of flour a tablespoon or two
of milk a teaspoon of baking powder a few drops of
essence of lemon.

❧ *Sally Lun* ❧

¾ lb flour   ¼ lb butter
2 eggs   tablespoonful baking powder
a little milk

Beat flour butter eggs with as much milk as will wet the flour. Add baking powder. Mix well together & put into a shape. Bake for ¾ hour in a moderate oven.

❧ *Yule Bread* ❧

[Traditionally, served to callers with a glass of wine. Lucas (1878) says this is the Scandinavian recipe – brought over by the Vikings to the upper dale.]

1½ lb plain flour   ¾ lb sugar
½ lb raisins   ½ lb currants
2 oz yeast   ¾ lb butter
2 oz candied peel   1½ teaspoon bicarbonate of soda
1 cup milk   1 tablespoon golden syrup
½ tsp nutmeg

Cream butter and sugar, add flour and fruit, warm the milk and mix with yeast, golden syrup and bicarbonate of soda. Add to the mixture. Put the mixture into two loaf tins and bake for 2 ½ hours at 350°F. Serve with butter.

8. The children's party, Methodist Manse, Dacre Bank (*c.*1900).

❧ *The Braisty Woods Christmas Cake* ❧

1¾ lb flour	½ lb candied lemon
2 lb currants	1 lb loaf sugar
1 lb butter	½ lb raisins
9 eggs	¼ lb chopped almonds
spices (nutmeg, allspice)	

Beat the butter by hand, work in the sugar, spices, eggs, flour and fruit.
[No cooking time given – assumes knowledge. Can be served with a slice of Coverdale cheese].

19th century

❧ *Simple Mincemeat* ❧

½ lb currants   ½ lb raisins
½ lb sultanas   1 lb apples
¼ lb beef suet   ½ lb brown sugar
¼ lb peel   2 oz almonds
spice to taste   1 wine glass of rum or brandy

❧ *Chancellor's Pudding* ❧

1 lb grated bread   1 quart milk boiled with
8 eggs   cinnamon & sugar
a little whiskey   nutmeg
a few raisins   few bits of sweet almonds
large tablespoon flour

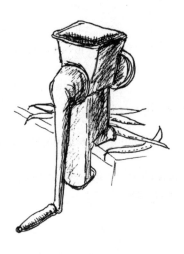

Pour boiled milk over bread, allow to steep. Beat eggs and add nutmeg, whiskey and almonds chopped very fine. Flour garnish inside of tin shape with raisins. Steam a little more than 1 hour. Sweeten to taste.

❧ *Apple Snow* ❧

Add to the pulp of 8 baked apples ½ lb powdered sugar, the juice of 1 lemon and the whites of 3 eggs. Whisk the whole for 1 hour, put some cream or custard in a dish and drop the whisked froth on it in large flakes. A pinch of alum makes the whisk firmer.

❧ *Apple Ginger* ❧

4 lbs sour apples	2 lbs sugar
4 lemons	1 oz white ginger root

Pare, core and chop apples; wash, remove seeds and chop lemons. Add sugar and ginger root and cook very slowly for five to six hours. Pour into jars and cover.

[JD notes '1927 Yorks. Fed. Women's Institutes 500 Recipes']

❧ *Apple and Pear Jam* ❧

2 lbs apples   4 lbs ripe pears
5 lbs sugar   [water]

Boil the apples with 2 lb sugar until tender. Then add pears and rest of sugar and boil until tender. Less sugar will do as the above is rather sweet.

Miss Watson

❧ *Seville Marmalade* ❧

Marmalade was popular as a dessert dish.
Seville oranges   water
Sugar (preserving is best)

Take Seville oranges and slice thinly, taking away the pips only. Add 3 pints of water to every 1 lb of sliced fruit, and let the whole stand for 24 hours. Next day boil till the peel is tender. Allow to stand in a bowl till the next day, when to every 1 lb of the mixture add 1 ½ lbs of sugar, and boil till the syrup ….. *[line missing, which is not untypical of JD's notes… 'reaches setting point'?…]*

❀ *Cherry And Walnut Jam* ❀

To 2 lb stoned cherries add 2 lbs sugar and juice of 2
oranges and 2 lemons. Boil gently, scum frequently, add
4oz each chopped walnuts and finely chopped raisins
when jam set.

❀ *Raspberry Jam* ❀

No water must be added; but still the fruit must be
boiled before adding the sugar.

4 lbs raspberries   4 lbs sugar

Place 4 lbs of fresh raspberries in a pan, cook over very
gentle heat till the juice runs, then simmer gently until
the fruit is tender. Add the sugar, stir. Boil rapidly till it
sets, about 2-3 minutes. Pot hot.

❧ *Marrow Jam* ❧

4 lbs marrow   juice of one lemon

3 lbs lump sugar   1½ oz bruised ginger.

Boil 2 or 3 hours.

❧ *Blackcurrant Jam* ❧

4 lbs blackcurrants   6 lbs sugar

3 pints water

Remove the stalks, wash the fruit and put into a preserving pan with the water. Simmer gently till the fruit is quite tender and the contents of the pan are reduced considerably. As the pulp becomes thick, stir frequently to prevent burning. Add the sugar, stir until it has dissolved, bring to a boiling point and boil hard until setting point is reached. Yield 10 lb.

[JD notes 'Yorkshire Way Y.F.W.T. Book']

❧ *Blackberry and Damson Cheese* ❧

8 lb blackberries   3 lbs damsons

1 pint water   sugar.

Wash fruit, put into pan with water, simmer. Rub through a sieve. Weigh the pulp add equal sugar and boil.

❀ *Marrow Cheese* ❀

4 lbs marrow steamed till quite tender, mash well, then add 4 lbs sugar, ½ lb butter and rind and juice of 4 lemons. Boil ½ hour.

❀ *Blackberry Jelly* ❀

Blackberries are plentiful in our dale hedgerows.
Put berries in a pan and a little over ½ cover with water. Bring to boil, simmer gently to extract juice. Add 1 or 2 apples washed and quartered but not peeled, to every pound of fruit. Strain. Boil 1 lb sugar to 1 pint of juice.

9. Hostel keepers at Scar House Village (*c.*1930).

❦ *Mint and Gooseberry Jelly* ❦

This makes a change from redcurrant jelly as an accompaniment to roast mutton.

To 4 lbs green gooseberries allow 2 pints water. Cook gently to a pulp. Rub through a sieve and to each pint of liquid allow 1 lb sugar; put into a preserving pan and add 30 stems of freshly gathered mint (tied in muslin). Boil till the jelly sets. Pot in small jars. If a brass pan is used for this recipe the jelly will be a nice green colour.

❦ *Green Gooseberry Jelly* ❦

3 lbs green gooseberries   2 pints water
6 lb sugar

Boil the gooseberries and water for 20 minutes, then add the sugar and boil vigorously for 5 minutes only, stirring all the time. In order to have the colour of the jam a light green when finished, it is essential that the fruit should not be boiled for a second longer than 5 minutes after the sugar has been added. A brass pan helps get a good colour.

[JD notes '1970 YFWI Book']

Stean Plums

Stean, famous for its gorge, is one of the most ancient settle-ments in the dale. Roman coins were found here; an early king of Scotland, founder of the Bayne family of Middlesmoor, hid here. The word is derived from 'Stan', old Norse meaning stone or rock. The Byland monks owned it for close on 400 years. 'Bakestanebec' was an area of woodland. They mention 'Great Stene Beck' 'Stene, Stane, Stan, Steinn, Stain.

The families of Stean form a very closely-knit community. Around the farmsteads are found plum trees peculiar to the area. The fruit is small, dark red, rather similar to the damson. The jam has a unique taste, rather sharp, but very pleasant. It is a feature of the Harvest Festival sales at Lofthouse and Middlesmoor Chapels. In a normal season they are ready for Pateley feast, but according to tradition they are better after they have had one mild frost on them.

It is unknown why these ancient trees are special to the area, but a number of them grow by Stean beck and in the gardens of local families. The Stean plum is bigger than a sloe. It is sour and bitter and needs a lot of sugar, but the jam is delicious with meats or on bread. Some put 2 lb sugar to 1 lb fruit. [But Dinah Lee recommends 1½ lb to avoid losing the distinctive tangy-ness. They were good keeping plums. Dinah's mother spread them on newspaper on the spare bedroom floor so they could be used in apple pies later in the winter.]

❧ *Stean Plum Jam* ❧

6 lbs Stean plums   6 lbs sugar
1½ pints of water

Simmer plums and sugar slowly, remove stones (kernels are good if cracked). Boil 10-15 minutes at a fast boil.

❧ *Stean Plum Conserve* ❧

6 lbs Stean plums   1 pt of water
lb sugar to each 1lb fruit pulp

Wash and stew plums gently, rub through a sieve. Weigh the pulp, add equal quantities of sugar, cook, stirring gently for approximately 20 minutes.

❧ *Red Tomato Sauce* ❧

6 lbs ripe tomatoes	pinch cayenne pepper
½ lb sugar	2 tablespoons tarragon vinegar
¾ oz salt	½ pint spiced vinegar
⅛ oz red paprika pepper	

Cut up the tomatoes and cook to a thick pulp. Run through a hair sieve, add the other ingredients, cook together until the consistency of thick cream. Bottle.

❧ *Dried Parsley* ❧

Pick the parsley in dry weather and put only the leaves on a baking tray lined with greaseproof paper. Put in a hot oven (not fan) with the door slightly ajar 425F for about 2 minutes. Remove dry leaves and crumble them. Some leaves might have to go back for another minute. Store in an airtight jar. This parsley stays green and will keep for years.

❧ *Pickled Damsons* ❧

To 1 pt. best vinegar add 3 quarts damsons and 3 lbs sugar.

Boil vinegar and sugar together, pour syrup over the damsons, strain and boil syrup again. Do this for 3 days. Then boil all together the third day for ½ hour gently. Then bottle.

1910

To Pickle Walnuts Green

Gather your walnuts when they are as you can run a pin through them, pare them and put in water, let them lye 4 or 5 days, stirring it twice a day to take out the bitter, then put them in strong salt and water, let them lye a week or ten days, stirring once or twice a day, then put them in fresh salt and water, and hang them over a fire, put to them a little alum, cover them up close with vine leaves, let them hang over a slow fire, whilst they be green, but be sure do not let them boil, when they are soft, put them into a sieve to drain the water from them.

To make a pickle for them, take a little good vinegar, put to it a little long pepper, and a few bay leaves, a little horse-radish, a handful of mustard seed, a little salt, a few shallots. Boil all in the vinegar, strain, put over the walnuts. Scald once a day for 3 or 4 days. Then tye down for use.

18th century

To Pickle Eggs

3 gallons water	9 tablespoons of Quick Lime
½ oz saltpetre	1 lb common salt

Boil and skim well, allow to stand 5 or 6 days stirring constantly.

The above will pickle 250 eggs – eggs should be put in fresh 2 or 3 dozen at a time.

From Miss J. Jenkins Book, early 19th century

❀ *Piccalilli* ❀

2 large cauliflowers	3 lbs shallots
3 lbs green tomatoes	2 quarts vinegar
1 lb sugar	¼ lb mustard
½ oz turmeric	1 small cupful flour

Prepare the vegetables and cut into small pieces. Place in a bowl with 4 quarts water and ½ lb salt. Mix well and stand overnight. Put into a pan, bring to the boil and cook for a few minutes. Remove and drain well in a colander. Put the vinegar in another pan, bring to the boil with the sugar. Mix the flour, mustard and turmeric into a smooth paste with a little water. Add some of the vinegar to the paste, stirring all the time. Then strain into the rest of the vinegar, stirring well. Again bring to the boil and boil for quite [*missing*] vegetable and again bring [*missing … It is difficult, as editor, to complete this. Those who knew her suggest that JD might have said 'Use your common sense.'*]

❧ *Mixed Herb Vinegar* ❧

To one quart of the best wine vinegar allow 1 oz each
of chives, shallots, tarragon, winter savoury and balm,
also a handful of mint. Pound the herbs well then add
to the vinegar in a bottle, cork well and place in the
sun every day for a fortnight. At the end of the fortnight strain well, squeezing the herbs at the same time.
Leave to settle for a few hours then re-strain through a
fine cloth and bottle.

10. Birstwith Band, Hardcastle Garth (*c.*1900).

NOVEMBER

At Hallowtide, slaughter-time entereth in,
And then doth the husbandman's feasting begin:
From thence unto Shrovetide, kill now and then some
Their offal for household the better will come.

❧ *Mint Sauce for Winter Use* ❧

Dissolve and boil 1 lb sugar in 1 pint best vinegar. Into a wide-necked jar put as much chopped mint as it will hold, pouring in the sweetened hot or cold vinegar as the jar is being filled. It should be fairly tightly packed. Green colouring may be added. A glass, plastic or bakelight top is best for the jar. Use as required by diluting with more vinegar.

[JD notes 'YWWI calendar for 1983']

Winter Tasks

For threshing forbear as ye may, till Candlemas coming; for sparing of hay.

Such wheat as ye keep for the baker to buy, unthreshed till March in the sheaf let it lie.

Set garlic and beans at St Edmund the King (Nov.20) the moon in the wane, thereon hangeth a thing

Salt the beef, sweep the chimney, trench the garden

❧ *Green Gooseberry Chutney* ❧

2 lbs green gooseberries	2 lbs sugar
1 lb raisins	1 lb dates
4 oz ground ginger	½ oz garlic
¾ oz chillies	2 oz salt
vinegar	

Top and tail gooseberries, put in pan with enough vinegar to cover and boil till soft. Stone and chop dates and raisins, add to the fruit. Add all other ingredients, boil for about 10 minutes. Bottle in the usual way.

❧ *Grandmother's Chutney* ❧

1 lb marrow	¼ oz ground ginger
1 lb red tomatoes	8 cloves
¼ lb green tomatoes	2 oz garlic
½ lb chopped onions	1 ½ oz salt
2 oz chopped shallots	¼ oz white pepper
½ lb preserving sugar	1 lb apples
½ lb sultanas	¼ oz pickling spice
1 pint vinegar	1 oz mustard seed

Peel, slice and cut marrow, apples and tomatoes, add
chopped onions and shallots and garlic, sultanas, salt,
sugar and spices (in spice bag tied to handle). Bring
all to the boil with the vinegar, simmer slowly till the
vinegar has been absorbed. Bottle immediately.

[JD notes 'YWWI calendar for 1983']

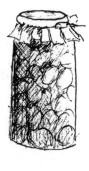

❧ *For Salting Beef* ❧

4 gallons water	4 lbs Bay Salt
2 oz Salt of Prunella	2 lbs brown sugar

Boil these together for 15 minutes and take all the skim that rises. When quite cold pour the liquor over the meat. All meat should be well rubbed with common salt before putting into the pickle.

❧ *Cucumber and Green Pickle* ❧

½ lb onions finely sliced   1 ½ lb ridge cucumber
½ teaspoon turmeric   1 green pepper (shredded)
¾ oz salt   1 level teaspoon mustard seed
½ teaspoon pimento   ½ pint distilled vinegar
¼ teaspoon mace   5 oz sugar
(½ teaspoon celery seed can be used instead of pimento)

Dice cucumber, remove seeds and membranes from the green pepper and dice. Put veg in bowl and mix with salt. Leave 2–3 hours. Drain, rinse in cold water, and drain again. Put in pan, add pickle ingredients, dissolve sugar, boil 2 minutes. Add drained veg and bring to boiling point again, stirring all the time. Put into jars, preferably small, and seal.

11. Mrs William Robinson on her milk float, Glasshouses.

❦ *Tonic Beetroot Wine* ❦

2 lbs beetroot   1 lb brown sugar
1 bottle Guiness Stout.

Wash beetroot, add sugar, stand 24 hours, squeeze through muslin and add stout. Stand 24 hours and bottle.

❈❖❈ ❖❈❖❈ ❖❈❖❈ ❖❈❖❈ ❖❈❖❈ ❖❈❖❈ ❖❈❖❈ ❖❈❖❈ ❖❈❖❈ ❖❈❖❈

The next 3 recipes are from a Recipe Book dating from
the 1840s belonging to Mrs Pawson, Hampsthwaite W.I.

❈❖❈ ❖❈❖❈ ❖❈❖❈ ❖❈❖❈ ❖❈❖❈ ❖❈❖❈ ❖❈❖❈ ❖❈❖❈ ❖❈❖❈ ❖❈❖❈

❃ *Ginger Wine* ❃

To 1 gallon of water: 4 oranges and 1 lemon, 3 ½ lbs
loaf or white sugar, 1 ½ oz white whole ginger. Peel
oranges and lemon very thin, take off all the white
and boil peel with sugar and ginger gently for about
1 hour. Pour it over the oranges and lemon into a pan.
The sugar will work it, skim and bottle when working.

❃ *Blackberry Syrup* ❃

Put the blackberries into a bowl and just nicely cover
them with boiling water. Let them stand for 24 hrs,
then strain off all the syrup you can. Use 1 lb sugar to
every quart of syrup and boil 20 minutes, flavour with
cloves, lemon and ginger.

❃ *Ginger Beer* ❃

1 gallon boiling water   1 lb loaf sugar
1 oz bruised ginger   cream of tartar or 1 large lemon
1 oz German yeast

Stand 12 hours, skim and bottle, do not overfill bottles.

*The following are all from a very old family book owned
by Miss J. Jenkins of Pateley Bridge.*

❧ *Cowslip Wine* ❧

To 5 gallons water add 18 lbs Loaf Sugar – Boil 20
minute – pare 5 lemons very thin, pour the boiling
liquor over the rinds when it is new milk warm. Add
5 gallons cowslips pips and 2 tablespoonsful of yeast
upon thick toast. The next day put in the juice of the
lemons and barrel it.

❧ *Blackberry Wine* ❧

Press juice from blackberries and allow to stand for 36
hours to ferment (lightly covered). Skim what rises to
the top. Then to every quart add ½ pint of water and 3
oz sugar. Let it stand covered for 24 hours, skim, strain
and bottle, keep 9 months.

❧ *Elder Wine* ❧

Put the berries into a jar and put them into a slow oven
all night, then mix 2 pints of the juice with 6 pints of
water. Add 4 lbs sugar, a little ginger and cloves. Boil
45 minutes and when cool ferment with yeast spread
upon toast, and let it work 2 days, then put it into a
cask, bung lightly till fermentation is over.

❧ *Dandelion Wine* ❧

'*This is an excellent home made wine.*'
To make 1 gallon: 2 pints dandelion blossom, 3 lb moist
sugar, ½ oz caraway seeds. Boil blossoms 20 minutes.
Boil sugar and seeds till clear. Pour it on to the peels
of 2 oranges and 1 lemon. Let it stand working 3 days
with yeast on toast. Then bottle, put the orange and
lemon peel into the cask.

June 1885

❧ *Rhubarb Wine* ❧

A very old recipe.
Take a good armful of rhubarb, break it into pieces.
Cover with 5 quarts of boiling water. Stir each day for
5 days, then strain and put in 4 lbs sugar, juice of 1
lemon and 1 lb of raisins, 1 oz Isinglass and a few raspberries. Let it stand 5 weeks. Keep a little of the liquor
to fill the cask as it ferments, then bottle off.

❧ *Verjuice [Crab Apple Juice]* ❧

Gather crabbes as soon as kernels turn blacke, lay in a
heap to sweat, take to the trough, crush with beetles.
Make a bagge of coarse haircloth, fill with crabbes and
presse. & run the liquor into hogsheads.

OCTOBER

T das gits short an t' neets er lang.
T' weather grows cawd an' chilly;
We creep roond t' fire, an' toke about
Life being' rough an' hilly.

❧ *Elderberry Syrup* ❧

Enough berries to fill a preserving pan to the top, with
    sufficient water to cover.
1 oz cloves   1 oz root ginger
½ lb sugar to each pint of liquid

Place the berries in the water and boil for one hour,
strain and press out all the juice. Bruise the spices and
tie in a muslin bag. Put the strained liquid back into the
preserving pan with the required amount of sugar and
the spices. Stir till the sugar dissolves. Boil for one hour,
and when cold, strain into bottles.

❧ *Lemonade* ❧

1½ lbs lump sugar   1 oz tartaric acid
1 quart boiling water

Pour boiling water over sugar. When cold add 1 dessertspoon of essence of lemon. Keep well corked. 1
tablespoonful to a glass of water. It is a splendid drink.

❧ *Temperance Brandy* ❧

15 to 20 grains of compound cinnamon powder in a wineglass of hot water.

[In JD's collection is a small booklet published by the Bradford District Union of the National British Women's Temperance Association, entitled Recipes for Temperance Drinks for Winter and Summer. Trifles and Sweets without Alcohol. Substitutes for Brandy, etc. *The introduction states that it was published 'in connection with their Exhibit at the Cartwright Memorial Exhibition' (Bradford, May 1904) and 'will supply a long-felt want amongst Temperance people [to enjoy] wholesome and harmless beverages [which] may be provided at small cost and with little trouble'. There are forty-three recipes in all. Here are three of them.]*

❧ *Drink For the Harvest or Hayfield* ❧

Four gallons boiling water, 1-lb. medium oatmeal, 1-lb. sugar, four lemons sliced, pour boiling water over these ingredients and stir well. Can be drunk either warm or cold.

12. Church 'Workers' Ladies, Middlesmoor.

❧ *Fruit Trifle* ❧

Place the pears from a tin in a trifle dish, take a pink jelly square, put in a basin, put the juice from the pears into a pint measure, fill up with water and make it hot enough to melt the jelly, when cool enough pour over the pears and let this set, make three gills of good custard, pour over, then finish with a layer of whipped cream, garnish with glacé cherries and angelica, or according to taste; coloured jelly looks best with pears, but apricots with yellow jelly is very nice.

❦ *Mrs Hibbert's Pick-Me-Up* ❦

Pour half a breakfastcupful of boiling water on as much cayenne pepper as would lie on a threepenny piece, sweeten to taste, add a good quantity of milk or cream.

❦❦❦

Furniture Polish

¼ pt turpentine   ¼ pt boiled linseed oil

⅛ pt vinegar   ⅛ pt methylated spirit

Pour the four liquids into a bottle and shake well before use. This polish is easily applied and is especially good for dark woods. If frequently used it is said to prevent wood from being worm eaten.

Bran Water

Bran water for washing coloured curtains: To every pint of water add one teacupful of bran. Boil for half an hour. Strain through a jelly bag. Use half a part of bran water to one part of water and a little soap jelly for washing the curtains. Rinse in equal parts and do not use starch. If colours run add salt and vinegar – 1 tablespoon to the quart. Makes cottons and coloured muslins look like new.

Anti-Moth Herbs

Equal parts of dried thyme and rosemary sprigs and catmint, with the addition of a few cloves, tied in muslin bags make good moth deterrents; and conkers on a windowsill keep out black spiders.

Pomanders

Perhaps one of the nicest ways of perfuming a room is to have in it a bowl of Pomanders. The name derives from the French 'pomme d'ambre' – apple of amber – and used to be a ball made of such perfume as ambergris or musk, which was carried in a perforated case, often of gold or silver and ornamented with jewels. Another form of pomander is made by sticking an orange (a Seville is particularly good) full of cloves. The cloves should be put in extremely closely so that the whole surface of the skin is covered. The orange can then be rolled in a mixture of cinnamon and orris root and a little cedar wood and sandalwood if available, wrapped in greaseproof paper and put in a very cool oven, or the airing cupboard for 2-4 weeks. Then unwrap and tie with red ribbon and hang in the wardrobe. They make very good presents.

Skin Moisturising Cream

3 tablespoons of soap flakes	1 tablespoon of glycerine
1 tablespoon of witch-hazel	4 tablespoons of olive oil

Mix the flakes in ¼ cup of water, then add glycerine and witch-hazel and warm until flakes are dissolved, then add olive oil. Pour into a jar which allows room for shaking, and shake well. Should make about 3 ozs, settling into a cream in about 24 hours. A few drops of perfume may be added, but not toilet water or eau de cologne.

> *[JD notes: This recipe was given to me by a very old friend some years ago now; she told me she originally heard it on the radio before the war.]*

Hand Cream

Mix to a smooth paste 10 grammes tragacanth with a spoonful of surgical spirit. Then stir in a bottle of glycerine (100ml.). Add ½ pint of boiling water, stirring quickly. If too thick add more water. Oil of lavender to perfume.

Soap Liniment

Equal parts of glycerine and opodeldoc.
For winter cracks at finger and thumb tips, frequently dab with soap liniment.

To Make Soap

3 lbs fat	½ lb caustic soda
1 ½ pints cold water	

Pour the water over the soda. Stir it well and allow it to cool a little. Melt the fat and cool it a little. Pour soda and water mix over the fat, which must not be too warm. Stir until the mixture looks like honey.

*From mid-November till mid-February dark days of mist
and rain, and sometimes heavy snows, take their toll and sap
the vitality of the strongest. Flu and colds and rheumatism
and lumbago claim many victims. The following remedies
have been collected locally.*

For Neuralgia
Sulphate of quinine sixteen grains, diluted sulphuric
acid half drachm, water 8-ozs. Take a tablespoonful in
half a wineglass of water three times a day after meals.

[From Recipes for Temperance Drinks
for Winter and Summer, *1904]*

For Cramps At Night
Put corks in the bed. Take a little salt with water.

A Gargle for Sore Throats
Small glass of Port wine   6 sage leaves
1 tablespoon of chilli vinegar 1 dessertspoon of honey

Simmer together on the fire for 5 minutes.

Liniment for a Bad Chest
Equal parts of oil of camphor, cloves and amber.

Cough Mixture

4 oz juniper berries

2 oz honey

1½ oz extract of
   sarsaparilla

2 oz Spanish juice

2 oz sugar candy

1 tablespoon linseed

2 quarts water

Add water to juniper berries and linseed, and simmer
down to 1 quart. Strain and add remainder of ingredients, boil for 10 minutes. When cold add ½ oz of
paregoric, and bottle for use. Dose a teaspoon when
cough is troublesome.

[From Recipes for Temperance Drinks
for Winter and Summer, *1904]*

Cough Cure

1 teaspoon honey	1 tablespoon glycerine
2 tablespoons lemon juice	2 teaspoons white Vaseline

Place in a mug in a saucepan of boiling water. Add 5 drops Friars Balsam. Bottle. Take a teaspoon at intervals.

13. Sheep Washing, Stean Moor (*c.*1908).

What is that which all love more than life
Fear more than death or mortal strife
That which contented men desire
The poor possess – the rich require
The miser spends, the spendthrift saves
And all men carry to the grave –

NOTHING

Conversion Table
and Abbreviations

These old recipes are almost entirely in imperial measurements. The following is approximate only. 1 oz = 28.352 grammes, but for practical purposes it is here taken as 30 grammes. The cup measurement is 225 grammes (8 oz) or for liquids 250 mls (10 fl oz).

Weights:

(approx)				
15	grammes	=	½	oz
30	'	=	1	'
50	'	=	1¾	'
60	'	=	2	'
75	'	=	2½	'
100	'	=	3½	'
500	'	=	1 lb 1½	'
1 kilo		=	2 lb 3	'

Liquid Measures:

(approx)			
1 litre	=	1¾ pts – 35 oz
1 decilitre	=	3-4 oz or 1 wineglass
1 demilitre	=	¾ pt (generous)

The
Nidderdale Museum

http://www.nidderdalemuseum.com/

Winner of the National Heritage Museum of the Year
Award 1990

Registered Charity Number 532339
Registered Museum Number 209

The Nidderdale Museum was founded in 1975 by a
group of enthusiasts who realised that much of the traditional life of the dale was quickly disappearing. The
premises are provided by Harrogate Borough Council
in the building originally erected as the Pateley Bridge
Union Workhouse (1863) to replace an earlier one
on Bishopside Moor. It is now known as The Old
Workhouse. Apart from this assistance, the museum is
entirely run and staffed by volunteers.

The Nidderdale Museum Society

Nidderdale Museum Society welcomes new members. As well as supporting the museum, it has its own programme of activities. There are monthly meetings throughout the winter with lectures on topics of local and general history interest. In addition, members may help in stewarding, preparing displays, and administrative work.

Address

The Old Workhouse,
Pateley Bridge,
Harrogate,
North Yorkshire,
HG3 5LE
Telephone: 01423 711225
Email: nidderdalemuseum@btconnect.com

Opening Times

Easter to 31 October: Daily 1.30 to 4.30 p.m.
School Summer Holidays and Bank Holiday Mondays:
10.30 am to 4.30 pm
Winter: Saturdays and Sundays only, 1.30 to 4.30 p.m.
Closed Christmas Day, Boxing Day and New Year's Day
Groups at any time by prior arrangement

Nidderdale AONB

The Nidderdale Area of Outstanding Natural Beauty (AONB) covers 233 square miles (603 km²) of Northern England in the county of North Yorkshire. The AONB shares a common boundary with the Yorkshire Dales National Park immediately to the west. The special quality of the landscape was formally recognised by the Government on 14 February 1994 when it was designated as an Area of Outstanding Natural Beauty.

Map reproduced with the kind permission of the Nidderdale Area of Outstanding Natural Beauty.

Overleaf 14. Map of Nidderdale, showing place-names mentioned.

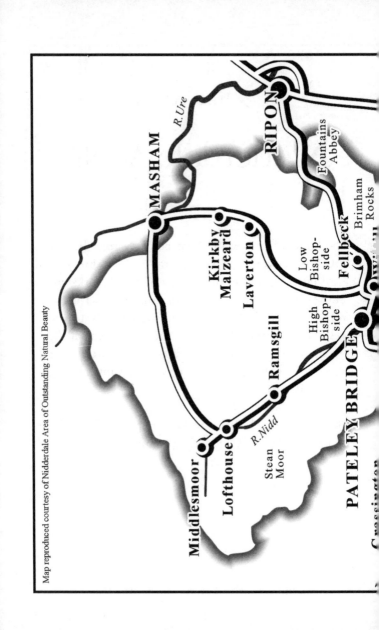

Map reproduced courtesy of Nidderdale Area of Outstanding Natural Beauty

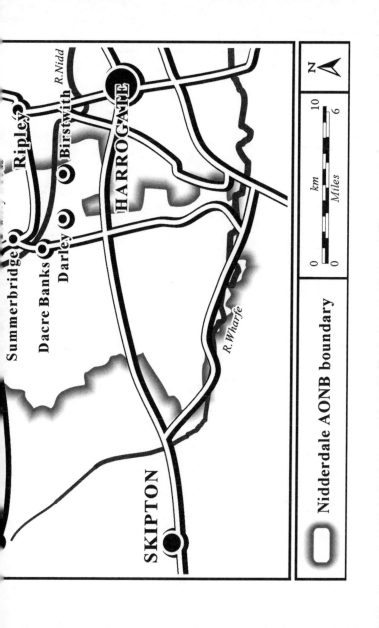

Ripley

R.Nidd

Summerbridge

Birstwith

Dacre Banks

Darley

HARROGATE

R.Wharfe

SKIPTON

N

0   km   10

0   Miles   6

Nidderdale AONB boundary

Select Bibliography

Manuscript Sources

Dawson, Joanna. Joanna's Recipe Collection: D*6627/6628/6638*. Nidderdale Museum Society.

Printed Sources

Alred, David. *Nidderdale Yesterday: A Pictorial Record of Life in a Dales Valley*. Smith Settle, 2001, p. 122–24.

Bradford District Union of the National British Women's Temperance Association. *Recipes for Temperance Drinks for Winter and Summer*. Exhibit at the Cartwright Memorial Exhibition, Bradford, 1904. Nidderdale Museum Ref. Joanna's Recipe Collection D*6638.3*.

Burgess, Eileen. 'Church and Chapel', Chapter 11 in Nidderdale Museum Society, *The Book of Nidderdale. Aspects of a Yorkshire Valley.* Halsgrove, 2003, p.113.

Dawson, Joanna, & Brown, Mrs Matthew. *Chapel Teas of Former Years: Favourite Recipes of Church Members Past and Present.* Lofthouse Methodist Church, 1982.

Hartley, Marie, & Ingleby, Joan. *Life and Tradition in the Yorkshire Dales. The Dalesman* Smith Settle, 1956.

Jennings, Bernard, ed. *A History of Nidderdale.* The Advertiser Press, Ltd, Huddersfield, 1967.

Lucas, Joseph. *Studies in Nidderdale: Upon Notes and Observations.* Eliot Stock, 1878.

Moody, Joanna. *Scar House Village.* Nidderdale Museum Society, 2009.

Associated websites
http://www.nidderdalemuseum.com/

http://www.nidderdale.co.uk/

http://www.nidderdaleaonb.org.uk/nidderdale-*0*

Index *of* Recipes

About *the* Author

Joanna Moody used to teach at the University of York. She has edited an Elizabethan diary and various collections of letters. Her most recent book was *From Churchill's War Rooms Letters of a Secretary 1943-45* (2007). Eileen Burgess is a local historian and former Primary School head teacher. Her most recent book was *Act Now! The Story of Pateley Bridge Dramatic Society* (2007). Sheila Hone is a painter and artist who has lived in Nidderdale for over forty years. Her illustrations are to be found in *The 1891 Project* (2007), a source book for Key Stage 2 children.

All three are retired, and are members and volunteer stewards at the Nidderdale Museum in the Yorkshire Dales.

Notes

Notes

Notes